ENGLiSH TALK

KMU AE Committee

Do You Speak English?

Keimyung University Press

Contents

★ Unit 1 • Introduction ★

Lesson 1 What's your name?

A Model Conversation

Read the conversation. Then listen. Track 01

Maya: Hello. Are you the tutor?

Martín: Yes, I am. Are you here for tutoring?

Maya: Yeah. Is it just me?

Martín: No, I have a list of seven names here. What's yours?

Maya: It's Maya.

Martín: Maya. Yep, right here. Your last name is Mandelli, right?

Maya: Yeah, that's me.

Martín: Great. My name's Martín, by the way. Martín Abreu.

B Vocabulary: People

Study the words. Then listen to the conversation again and fill in the blanks. Track 01

girl

boy

woman

man

← People

People at school →

student

teacher

classmates

tutor

1. Maya is the ⓐ __________. She is a ⓑ __________. Her ⓒ __________ name is Mandelli.
2. The ⓐ __________ is Martín. His last ⓑ __________ is Abreu. He is a ⓒ __________.
3. They ⓐ __________ not ⓑ __________.

C Grammar

Simple present: *be*

Brief note

Use *he* for a man, *she* for a woman, and *it* for a thing.

be questions	answers to *be* questions	*be* statements
Am I a student?	✓ Yes, you **are** (a student).	You**'re** a student.
Are you a teacher?	✗ No, I**'m not** (a teacher).	I**'m not** a teacher.
Is he a man?	✓ Yeah (, he**'s** a man).	He**'s** a man.
Are we classmates?	✗ Nope (, you**'re not** classmates).	You**'re not** classmates.
Are you girls?	✓ Yep (, we**'re** girls).	We**'re** girls.
Are they friends?	✗ No, they **aren't** (friends).	They **aren't** friends.

Brief note

Yep, *yeah*, and *nope* are informal. Use them with your friends.

D Grammar Practice

Write *be* questions. Then circle *yes* or *no* and fill in the blanks.

1. Q: ____________ you John? A: (Yes / No), ____________ Daniel.
2. Q: ____________ you teachers? A: (Yes / No), ____________ are teachers.
3. Q: ____________ he your boss? A: Yes, ____________ is my ____________.
4. Q: Are ____________ our teacher? A: Yes, I'm ____________ teacher.
5. Q: Is ____________ your dog? A: No. ____________ a cat.

E In Your World

Look at the name tags. Write your first name and last name on a tag. Then choose a partner. Ask his or her name and design a name tag for him or her.

What is your name?

HELLO!
My name is

What is your partner's name?

HELLO!
My name is

F Use the Language

Introductions

1. Think of your first meeting with an important person—a friend, your boyfriend or girlfriend, your boss, etc. Write the first conversation between you and that person.

A: ____________________

____

B: ____________________

____

A: ____________________

____

B: ____________________

____

2. Choose a partner. Role-play your conversation.

MEMO

Lesson 2 Titles

A Model Conversation

Read the conversation. Then listen. Track 02

Angela: Hello, Mr. Garza.
Jimmy: Oh. Hi, Miss Wells. Please call me Jimmy.
Angela: Okay, then you can call me Angela.
Jimmy: All right. And how are you today, Angela?
Angela: I'm good, Jimmy. What about you?
Jimmy: Yeah, I'm okay, too. Is the teacher here?
Angela: Mrs. Watson? I don't know. I don't see her.

B Vocabulary

Study the words and phrases. Listen and repeat. Then try to add more jobs. Track 03

Marital status

married

single

Jobs

doctor

professor

truck driver

police officer

Other jobs

C Vocabulary: Titles

man: Mister (Mr.) **woman:** Ms.
married woman: Mrs. **unmarried woman:** Miss

medical doctor or PhD: Doctor (Dr.)
university professor: Professor (Prof.)

Listen and practice. Track 04

1. Mr. & Mrs. Smith
2. Prof. Alvarez
3. Ms. Green
4. Dr. Jones
5. Miss Perkins

D Grammar

Short forms (contractions) in negative statements

<table>
<tr><th colspan="2">short forms in negative statements</th></tr>
<tr><td>I'm not</td><td>we're not / we aren't</td></tr>
<tr><td>you're not / you aren't</td><td>you're not / you aren't</td></tr>
<tr><td>he's not / he isn't</td><td rowspan="3">they're not / they aren't</td></tr>
<tr><td>she's not / she isn't</td></tr>
<tr><td>it's not / it isn't</td></tr>
</table>

E Grammar Practice

Fill in the blanks with a short form or a title.

1. I'm Jimmy. I'm a student. ________ ________ a truck driver.

2. Angela Wells is single. S________ ________ married. ________ Wells is a student.

3. The teacher is a woman. S________ ________ a man. ________ married. Her name is ________ Watson.

F About You

Fill out the first part of a visa application form.

What country are you going to?

____

VISA APPLICATION

Visa application time: 9:00–11:00 a.m. M-F
Visa pick-up time: 11:00 a.m.–12:00 p.m. M-F

Part 1: Personal Information

Title Mr. ___ Mrs. ___ Miss ___ Ms. ___

Marital Status Single ___ Married ___ Divorced ___ Widow(er) ___ Other ___

Name Given Name (First Name)	Surname (Family Name)

G Use the Language

Introducing other people

1. Give the people names, jobs, and titles. Are they married?

First name: ______________
Last name: ______________
Marital status: ______________
Job: ______________
Title: ______________

Name: ______________
Surname: ______________
Married? Yes / No
Occupation: ______________
Title: ______________

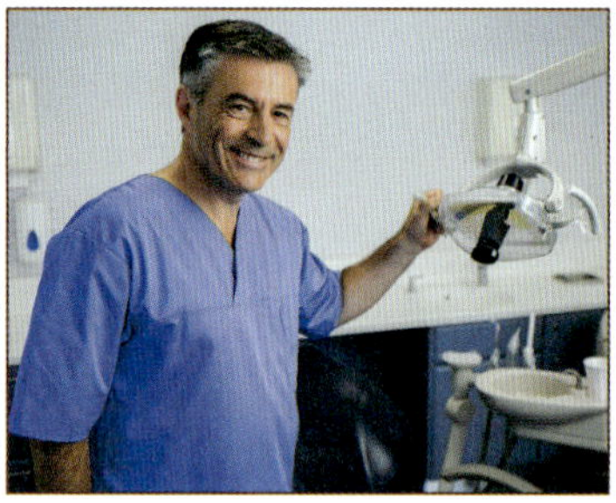

Given name: ______________
Family name: ______________
Married / Unmarried
Career: ______________
Title: ______________

2. Choose a partner. Take turns introducing the people above to your partner. Use affirmative and negative statements.

3. Write an introduction about one of your partner's people.

____

____

____

____

____

MEMO

Lesson 1 Talking About the Weekend

A Model Conversation

Read the conversation. Then listen. Track 05

Anna: Hey, Paolo. How was your weekend?

Paolo: It was great. How about yours?

Anna: Not bad. I looked after my friend's son on Saturday. He's a good kid, but he acted up a lot. I looked up lots of activities on the Internet to try and keep him busy.

Paolo: That sounds stressful. I dropped Natalia off at the airport on Saturday. Then I just listened to music on the balcony and went to bed early. I relaxed all day Sunday, too.

Anna: That sounds nice. On Sunday I wanted to do something relaxing, too, so I called up some friends to go dancing.

Paolo: That sounds like fun!

B Vocabulary

Read the conversation again. Write *A* next to the activities that Anna did and *P* next to the ones that Paolo did. Put an *X* next to activities Anna and Paolo did not do. Then match the expressions to the correct definitions.

1. ____ look after •
2. ____ act up •
3. ____ look up •
4. ____ drop (someone) off •
5. ____ kick (someone) out •
6. ____ look in on •

- • **a.** to remove (someone) from a place because of bad behavior
- • **b.** to find information
- • **c.** to take care of
- • **d.** to behave badly
- • **e.** to check whether someone is okay
- • **f.** to drive (someone) to a place and leave him or her there

C Grammar

Simple past (regular verbs) and past time expressions

simple past (regular verbs): verb + *-ed*		
statements	**negatives**	**yes/no questions**
I He / She / It **watched** TV. We / You / They	I He / She / It **did not watch** TV. We / You / They **(didn't)**	**Did** I he / she / it **watch** TV? we / you / they

past time expressions			
yesterday	last week(end) / month / year	last Friday	two days / weeks / months / years ago

Brief note

Except for the verb *be*, in the simple past, verb forms are the same for all subjects.

D Grammar Practice

Make sentences using an item from each column. Change the verbs to the simple past.

subject	verb	past time expression
Rinaldo Jacques and Helen My sister	cook dinner in the kitchen watch a movie in the living room clean the bathroom listen to the radio in the bedroom call his/her mother	yesterday last Monday three days ago last night two weeks ago

1. ______________________________

2. ______________________________

3. ______________________________

4. ______________________________

5. ______________________________

E Vocabulary Comprehension

Fill in the blanks with the correct forms of the phrases from part B.

1. The teacher ______________ ______________ students who don't listen in class.
2. My mother always ______________ ______________ on my brother when he is doing homework.
3. My dog never ______________ ______________ when we go to the park.
4. My mother ______________ me ______________ at school on her way to work.
5. I use the dictionary to ______________ ______________ words I don't know.
6. My best friend ______________ ______________ her litter sister on the weekends.

F Use the Language

When did you do...?

Find a partner.

Ask your partner questions using past time expressions. Make notes about his or her answers in the box.

Find out what your partner did...

yesterday
three days ago
last night
last weekend
last year

Share your partner's answers with the class.

MEMO

Lesson 2 It's a really nice day.

A Model Conversation

Read the conversation. Then listen. Track 06

Brief note

"What's up?" is a casual greeting similar to "How are you?" A common answer is, "Not much."

Jessica: Hi, Ben.
Ben: Hey, Jessica. What's up?
Jessica: Not much. You?
Ben: Uh, well, exams start next week. I like to study out here on the grass.
Jessica: Great idea. It's a really nice day. It's very sunny, though.
Ben: Oh, I usually sit under a tree so I don't feel hot. Sometimes there are empty benches in the shade.
Jessica: Ah, that sounds nice.
Ben: Do you want to join me?
Jessica: Well, I should be going. I have a really big test, too. But I usually study in my dorm.
Ben: Okay. Well, have a good day. Enjoy the weather.
Jessica: You too! Talk to you later.

B Vocabulary

Study the words and phrases. Then listen and repeat. Track 07

courtyard

dorm/ residence

flowers/ flower bed

bench

sidewalk/ walking path

Which of the things above can be found on your university campus? Where are they?

C Vocabulary: Weather

Listen and practice saying the weather phrases. Track 08

 It's sunny. The sun is out/shining.

 There's a storm. It's stormy.

 It's windy.

 It's cloudy.

 It's foggy.

 It's hot. It's warm.

 It's rainy. It's raining.

 It's snowy. It's snowing.

 It's cold. It's cool.

D Grammar

Intensifiers

We use intensifiers to make words stronger. We can put them before adjectives and adverbs.

really/very/so + adjective		
subject + *be* verb	**intensifier**	**adjective**
It's	**really**	sunny.
	very	hot.
	so	windy.

Brief note

So is used this way only in casual speaking and writing, not in formal writing.

Very and *really* can also be used between an article and an adjective before a noun.

really/very + adjective + noun				
subject + *be* verb	**article**	**intensifier**	**adjective**	**noun**
He's	a	**very**	smart	professor.
It's		**really**	nice	day.

E Grammar Practice

Put the words in order to make sentences.

1. person / very / a / kind / Marie / is

   ______________________________.

2. are / these / nice / flowers / so

   ______________________________.

3. is / hot / classroom / really / our

   ______________________________.

4. very / my / old / dorm / is

   ______________________________.

Rewrite the sentences with intensifiers to make them stronger and more descriptive.

5. The campus is big.

   ______________________________.

6. The trees on campus are tall.

   ______________________________.

F Quick Review

Find words or phrases that mean...

...food is really good: ____________ ...announcement board: ____________ ____________

...something doesn't cost anything: ____________ ..."How are you?": ____________ ____________

G Listen to Write

Listen to a woman describing her favorite place to spend time outdoors. Which place is she describing? Track 09

Think of an outdoor place where you like to spend time. Write a description. Then tell a partner.

____

____

____

____

____

MEMO

Lesson 1 Go traveling!

A Authentic Text: An online chat

Read the chat. What kind of vacation does the woman want to take?

Brief note

A "national park" is an area of land owned by the government because it is important to nature, history, or science.

Carrier

< Back

Damian 23: So, what are you going to do on your vacation? Have you ever thought about **sailing** around the world or **climbing** mountains?

Jules 21: No, too hard! I haven't decided yet, but I've always wanted to go backpacking or **sightseeing** in the US. I've never had a real adventure. But I still need some time to figure out where I'm going and what I'm going to do.

Damian 23: Volunteering abroad is another idea. Some of my friends **helped out** in a national park: cleaning up **litter** and **planting** trees. They had an amazing time. You can search for programs on the web.

Jules 21: I'll look into that. Volunteering may be an interesting thing to do, and I'm always on the Internet at night. I never go to bed before 1 a.m. It will give me something to research. I like the idea of traveling and doing something good for nature.

Damian 23: Yeah. A project like cleaning beaches or helping in a zoo is cool. Do you ever watch nature shows on TV? I love them. I've always wanted to swim with **dolphins**. Anyway, don't forget to **post** your photos during your vacation!

Message OK

Read the messages again. Put a check mark next to the true sentences.

1. ☐ He likes watching TV shows about nature.
2. ☐ She is never on the Internet at night.
3. ☐ She's always wanted to take a boat trip.
4. ☐ His friends had a bad time while they were volunteering.
5. ☐ She's been on exciting trips before.
6. ☐ She's going to think while she is traveling.
7. ☐ They're both interested in doing something good for nature.
8. ☐ He wants to see pictures of her trip.

B Vocabulary

Read the chat again. With a partner, match each bold word to its correct definition.

1. ____________ visiting the famous places in a specific location
2. ____________ volunteer one's help
3. ____________ to put (a message, photo, etc.) on a website for others to see
4. ____________ putting plants into the ground to grow

Write the correct bold word from the chat under each picture.

5. ____________

6. ____________

7. ____________

8. ____________

C About You

What have you always wanted to do while traveling? Think about three activities—places to visit, food to eat, people to meet, etc. Tell other students about them. What do they think about your ideas?

D Grammar

ever*, *never*, and *always*; *while* and *during

Brief note

Use *ever* only in questions and negative statements.

simple present with *ever* / *never* / *always*	present perfect with *ever* / *never* / *always*
You can use *ever*, *never*, and *always* with the present perfect to talk about people's past experiences. We also use them with the simple present to talk about people's lives now.	
Do you **ever** watch nature shows on TV? I **never** go to bed before midnight. She is **always** on the Internet at night.	Have you **ever** thought about sailing? I've **never** had a real adventure. She has **always** wanted to travel.
during + noun	*while* + clause
Both *during* and *while* communicate that something is happening at the same time as another thing. The preposition *during* is followed by a noun, but the conjunction *while* is followed by a clause (subject + verb).	
What do you enjoy doing **during** your time off? Post your photos **during** your vacation!	I'll figure out what I want **while** I'm traveling. Please write to me **while** you're abroad.

Brief note

In the present perfect, *ever*, *never*, and *always* come before the past participle.

E Grammar Practice

Circle the correct words to complete the short conversations.

1. A: Do you (ever / never / while) eat lunch on campus?
B: Yes, I do. I usually eat outside (during / always / while) I do my homework.

2. A: Have you (during / ever / while) had a job?
B: Yes, I have. I worked in a bookstore (ever / while / during) the summer.

3. A: Have you (while / during / ever) been to New York?
B: No, I've (always / ever / never) been there. But I'd love to go.

4. A: Do you ever fall asleep (while / during / never) you're in class?
B: No, I've never fallen asleep (while / during / ever) a class.

5. A: I've (ever / never / always) gone sailing. Have you?
B: Yes, once. My family rented a boat (while / during / ever) a trip to California.

6. A: What would you like to do (while / during / always) you're in Japan?
B: I've (ever / always / never) wanted to climb Mt. Fuji.

F Use the Language

Find out about your classmates.

Do some research on your classmates. First, choose a topic. Then, on a separate piece of paper, write a questionnaire (a list of questions) to ask the other students in your class. The topic could be on places in town, unusual foods, visiting tourist sites, dangerous activities, or your own idea. Make all of the questions yes/no questions.

Find out three students' information. Then write a paragraph about each of the students you interviewed.

MEMO

Lesson 2 Part-time Job

A Model Conversation

Read the conversation. Then listen. Track 10-1

Brenda: Oh, A.C.—nice to see you! How long have you worked here?

A.C.: Since school finished. So, since December. I'm taking next semester off, so I wanted a temporary job.

Brenda: What's it like?

A.C.: Well, the hours and the wages aren't bad, and I like the work so far.

Brenda: You're a friendly guy, so I'm sure you're good at customer service. Have they made you the boss yet?

A.C.: Haha. No, but I get some good tips. And they've made me assistant manager.

Brenda: Congratulations! How long have you had that position?

A.C.: Three weeks. The manager doesn't know much about computers, so I think he chose me for my IT skills.

Brenda: So far, it sounds great. Are you going to quit when you go back to school?

A.C.: I might stay. The company provides chances for advancement. I'm learning about organization and leadership. Maybe I'll get a higher-level job with this company after graduation.

Brief note

Some people abbreviate long names. "A.C." can stand for names such as "Anthony Carter."

Brief note

A "tip" is extra money that customers give when an employee does a good job of helping them.

Brief note

"provide" something is to give it to someone or make it available.

B Vocabulary

List four items for each category below. Use words from part B, words from previous units, and your own ideas. Share your answers with a partner.

advancement leadership customer service organization IT skills wages

Working Conditions	Work Skills

C About You

Below are some common jobs that college students do. Work with a partner. Write down other common jobs that students do.

pizza delivery person	babysitter	waiter	tutor	cashier

- ______________ • ______________ • ______________ • ______________
- ______________ • ______________ • ______________ • ______________
- ______________ • ______________

Which of these jobs have you had before? Which would you like to do? Why? Discuss your answers with your partner.

D Grammar

How long questions with the present perfect; *so far*

How long + present perfect questions	
Use *how long* + present perfect to ask about the period of time something has lasted, from the beginning until now. The answer often uses *since* or *for*.	
A: **How long** have you worked there?	B: **Since** school finished. / **For** three weeks.

so far	
So far means "up until now." We use it when we expect an action to continue. It usually comes at the beginning or the end of a sentence.	
I like the work **so far**. / **So far**, I like the work.	It sounds great **so far**. / **So far**, it sounds great.

Brief note

Like *yet*, *so far* talks about the time before now, but *yet* is only used in negatives and questions; *so far* can be used in any kind of sentence.

E Grammar Practice

Put the words in order to make sentences.

1. long / he / has / how / games / computer / played

____?

2. lived / you / long / have / how / there

____?

3. has / she / the / been / assistant manager / long / how

____?

4. I / so / my / love / far / new / job

____.

F Comprehension

Listen to the conversation. Circle true or false. Track 10-2

1.	Tara is running a restaurant downtown.	true	false
2.	The working conditions at her job are good so far.	true	false
3.	Tara has never done this kind of work before.	true	false
4.	She says that people need good IT skills for this job.	true	false
5.	She thinks she'll make a lot of money in her new job.	true	false

G Use the Language

Write about one of the activities. Then share your answers with other students and ask them about theirs.

Option 1: Choose a TV program you watch a lot. Write a few sentences about what has happened on the show recently, or since it started. What do you like about it?

Option 2: Describe a book or comic you're reading these days. Write a few sentences about how long you've read it, what's happened so far, and why you like it.

Option 3: Choose a video game you play a lot. Write a few sentences about how long you've played it, what's happened so far (best level, score, etc.), and why you like it.

MEMO

⋆ Unit 4 · Fitness and Health ⋆

Lesson 1 We'd better show up early.

A Model Conversation

Read the conversation. Then listen. Track 11

Hailey: Hey, Ben. You weren't in class yesterday—were you sick?

Ben: No, I'm fine. I went to cheer for my brother Ethan's college basketball team. It was such an excellent game.

Hailey: Oh, yeah? What happened?

Ben: They were behind by one point, and there were five seconds left. Then Ethan got the ball and scored. It was incredible.

Hailey: Wow! So, I guess your brother's a good player?

Ben: The best on the team—and it's a good team. I highly recommend you go and watch sometime. In fact, I'm going to their game on Wednesday, if you're free.

Hailey: I am. What time?

Ben: It starts at 7:00 p.m., but we'd better show up early to get good seats. Can you meet me here at 6:15?

Brief note

Use the preposition "on" to talk about being part of a team.
My friend Claire is ***on*** *that team.*

B Vocabulary

Write the words from the box next to the correct definitions.

basketball	excellent	show up	left	score	second	behind

1. ______________ to get a point or points in a game
2. ______________ 1/60 of a minute
3. ______________ to arrive at a place
4. ______________ having fewer points than the other person or team in a game
5. ______________ extremely good; fantastic
6. ______________ a sport in which players score by throwing a ball through a net (basket)
7. ______________ not used or finished yet; remaining

Match the parts to make sentences.

8. I waited for her for an hour, but she didn't •
9. Oh, we missed the game. There's only •
10. They're not going to win. They're behind •
11. If you're very tall, people might think you're •
12. I suggest you ask Rita to be on your team. She's •
13. Our basketball team played well. We scored •

- • **a.** by twenty-two points.
- • **b.** an excellent athlete.
- • **c.** ninety points.
- • **d.** one minute left.
- • **f.** show up.
- • **g.** good at basketball.

C About You

Are you punctual? Do you arrive early to events or are you always late? Talk to a partner about your time management skills.

D Grammar

Suggestions and advice with gerunds, infinitives, modals, and *that* clauses

suggestions and advice with gerunds and infinitives	
I suggest / I recommend + gerund	
*I **recommend watching** the basketball game on TV.*	*I **suggest going** on the weekend.*
Using *I suggest/recommend* + gerund sounds more formal than using infinitives or modal verbs.	
be sure / it's a good idea + infinitive	
Be sure to go to a game.	**It's a good idea to get** tickets early.
strong advice with the modal *had better*	**suggestions with *that* clauses**
subject + (*had*) *better* + verb	*I suggest/recommend* + *that* clause
We'**d better show up** early to get good seats. = We **better show up** early to get good seats.	I **recommend (that)** she go and watch the game. = I **suggest (that)** she go and watch the game.

Brief note

Informally, people often leave out *had*.

Brief note

In the *that* clause, use the base form of the verb with all subjects:
(✓) *I suggest (that) she/he/it go...*
(X) *I suggest (that) she/he/it goes...*

E Grammar Practice

Fill in the blanks with the correct words from the box.

better	idea	sure	suggest	bring	inviting	that

1. I ____________ that you stay. There are only ten minutes left in the game.
2. Be ____________ to see the college volleyball team sometime!
3. You'd better ____________ a warm coat. It's going to be cold later.
4. I recommended ____________ lots of friends to the game.
5. It's a good ____________ to watch the game on TV.
6. I recommend ____________ we sit near the front.
7. Jim's team had ____________ practice more. They never win any games.

F Suggestions

Read each person's comment. Then write one or two suggestions for each.

My family needs to spend more time together.

____

____

I can't concentrate on my schoolwork.

____

____

My friend and I had an argument.

____

____

MEMO

Lesson 2 It's very painful.

A Model Conversation

Read the conversation. Then listen. Track 12

Brief note

"What's the matter?" means "What's wrong?"

Trainer: What's the matter, Miguel? Did you hurt your shoulder?

Miguel: Yeah, I tried to lift that 40 kg weight pretty fast. I guess that wasn't smart. It really hurts.

Trainer: Uh-oh. Can you lift your arm?

Miguel: Yeah. I can, but it's very painful.

Trainer: Okay, then stop moving it. It might get even worse. I'll get a bandage. Then you'd better go home and put ice on it.

Miguel: Is that necessary? Maybe the pain will stop.

Trainer: No, it's possible that it's a serious injury. Rest the arm and take some pain relievers. If it isn't a lot better after three days, you'll need to see a doctor.

Brief note

The verb "put" needs two things after it: a direct object and an adverb or a prepositional phrase of location.
(✓) *Put ice on your shoulder. / Put ice there.*
(X) *Put ice.*

B Vocabulary

Match the words with the correct definitions.

1. shoulder •	• **a.** frozen water
2. serious •	• **b.** causing (a part of the body) to hurt
3. painful •	• **c.** possibly dangerous
4. put •	• **d.** a long piece of cloth to cover a hurt part of the body
5. pain reliever •	• **e.** medicine for making pain stop
6. bandage •	• **f.** the top of the arm
7. ice •	• **g.** the act of getting hurt; damage to part of the body
8. injury •	• **h.** to cause to be in a specific place

C Vocabulary: Body parts

Fill in the empty blanks with words from the box.

ankle	elbow	knee	neck	wrist	forehead

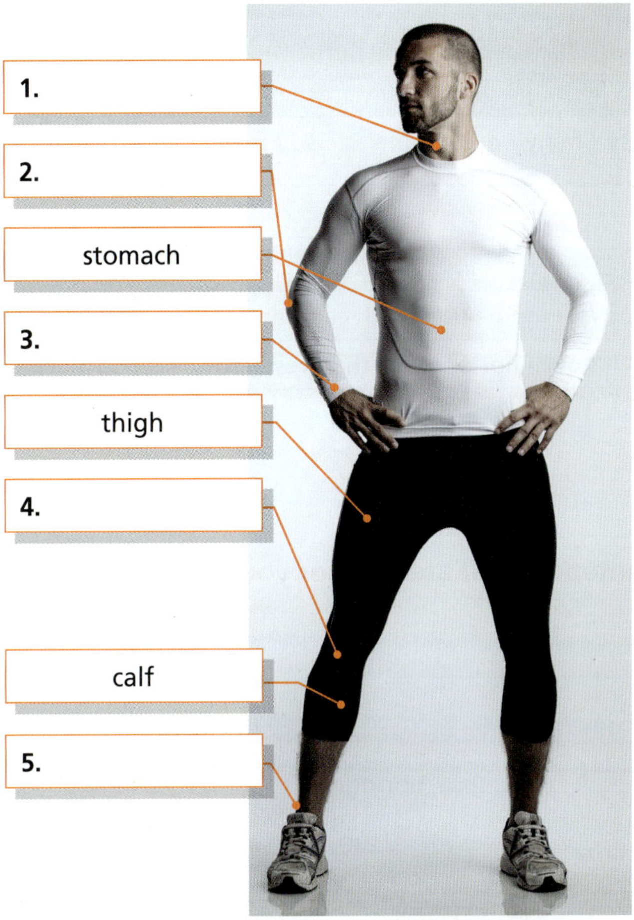

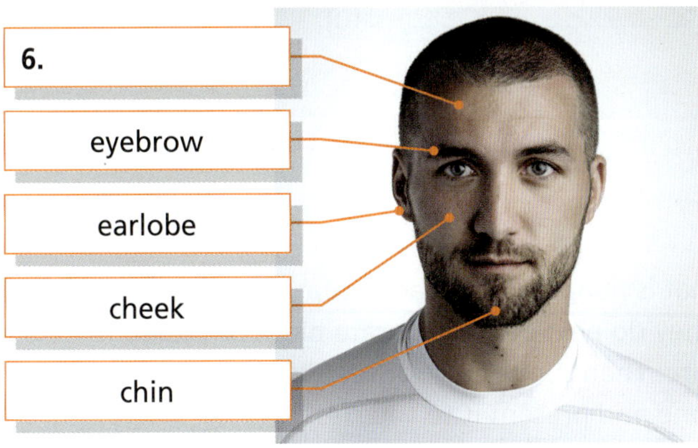

D About You

Think of a time you were injured. What did you hurt? How did the injury happen? Was it painful? What did you do about it? Tell your partner.

Brief note

Most of these intensifiers can be used in front of an adjective + noun. However, *a bit, a little,* and *so* cannot. They can only be used in front of an adjective alone.
(✓) *It's a **pretty** expensive gym.*
(✓) *It's **a bit** expensive.*
(X) *It's a bit expensive gym.*

E Grammar

Intensifiers

<table>
<tr><th colspan="4">intensifiers</th></tr>
<tr><td colspan="4">Use intensifiers to make the meaning of adjectives stronger. Sometimes you want to emphasize how big, small, great, painful, etc., something is. The intensifier can be a word or a phrase. It comes before the adjective:
Their house is really big.   The soup is a little salty.   Rock climbing is quite difficult.</td></tr>
<tr><th colspan="4">common intensifiers</th></tr>
<tr><td>a bit / a little</td><td>pretty / fairly / quite</td><td>so / really / very / super</td><td>extremely</td></tr>
<tr><td colspan="4"><---></td></tr>
<tr><td>least strong</td><td></td><td></td><td>strongest</td></tr>
<tr><th colspan="4">comparing using intensifiers</th></tr>
<tr><td colspan="4">Some intensifiers (even, so much, a lot) can be used with comparative adjectives. Other intensifiers cannot.</td></tr>
<tr><td colspan="4">My elbow feels a lot better now.   It's even hotter today than yesterday.   He's so much taller than his brother.</td></tr>
</table>

F Grammar Practice

Add an intensifier to make sentences that are true for you. Share with a partner. Do you and your partner agree?

1. Working out every day is ____________________ hard.
2. Cooking healthy meals every day is ____________________ difficult.
3. Cleaning the house is ____________________ boring.
4. Watching the Olympics is ____________________ fun.
5. Reading comic books is ____________________ relaxing.
6. Going on a blind date is ____________________ stressful.

G Use the Language

What's the matter?

Look at the pictures. Imagine what is happening in each situation. What problems do the people in the pictures have and what should they do next? On a separate piece of paper, write a conversation between you and the person in each picture. Then show your conversations to a partner. Practice the conversations together. Then choose the best one and present it to the class.

MEMO

⋆ Unit 5 · Out of Town ⋆

Lesson 1 Table for Two

A Model Conversation

Read the conversation. Then listen. Track 13

Pierre: Where do you want to go to celebrate your birthday on Friday?

Teresa: Well, I heard there's a terrific new Thai restaurant on Packard Avenue. It's called Sunset Thai.

Pierre: Oh, yeah. It gets really good reviews online. Amazing food. Great service. Beautiful décor.

Teresa: I know. Everyone is raving about it!

Pierre: I heard that the chef at Sunset Thai used to work at The Spice Restaurant.

Teresa: Then the food will be delicious for sure! And I heard the patio is gorgeous.

Pierre: Let's make a reservation right now, in case it gets fully booked.

Teresa: Okay. Table for two for Friday at 7 p.m. On the patio, of course!

B Vocabulary

Match each word with the correct definition.

1. celebrate •	• **a.** to talk about how wonderful something is
2. terrific •	• **b.** a waiter or waitress
3. server •	• **c.** to do something special for an important event
4. décor •	• **d.** an outdoor area attached to a home or restaurant
5. rave •	• **e.** very good; excellent
6. chef •	• **f.** extremely beautiful
7. patio •	• **g.** how the inside of a building looks: the furniture, pictures on the walls, etc.
8. gorgeous •	• **h.** a professional cook

C Vocabulary Comprehension

Circle the correct answers.

1. It's too cold to sit out on the (décor / patio) tonight.

2. The menu is completely different. Maybe they hired a new (server / chef).

3. The service at that new Italian place is (gorgeous / terrific).

4. I love the (décor / server) here. It feels like we're actually in a restaurant in Paris.

5. We're here to (rave / celebrate) my sister's graduation.

6. We're ready to order. Where is our (server / chef)?

7. My friend Celine recommends getting the seafood pasta. She just (raves / celebrates) about it.

D Grammar

Reported speech with *I heard*

Brief note
You may use the word *that* after *I heard*. This is optional.

reported speech with *I heard*	
Reported speech using *I heard* does not focus on where the information came from, so it is less reliable or trustworthy.	Other reported speech focuses more on where the information came from and is generally more reliable and trustworthy.
I **heard that** the new Italian restaurant is awful! We **heard** there's a big sale at the bookstore today. Jason said he **heard** there's a party at Tatiana's tonight. **Did** you **hear that** Maryanne got a new boyfriend?	I read a really bad online review of the new Italian restaurant. We got an ad in the mail about a big sale at the bookstore. Tatiana invited Jason to a party at her apartment tonight. Did Maryanne tell you that she got a new boyfriend?

E Grammar Practice

Put a check mark next to the correct description of each statement.

1. Fred told me that he is leaving the company. ☐ more reliable ☐ less reliable
2. I heard the pizza place on the corner is closing. ☐ more reliable ☐ less reliable
3. We heard that going downtown is dangerous. ☐ more reliable ☐ less reliable
4. *The York Daily* said the celebration is canceled. ☐ more reliable ☐ less reliable
5. My professor told me that there's a meeting on Monday. ☐ more reliable ☐ less reliable
6. I heard Martin and Hawa are getting a divorce. ☐ more reliable ☐ less reliable

F Use the Language

What have you heard about this restaurant?

Think of three restaurants in your town that are known by name to most of your classmates. (You may or may not have eaten at these places yourself.) List them on the left in the table below.

Restaurant	Person #1	Person #2	Person #3
1.			
2.			
3.			

Now ask three classmates about the restaurants. They may give their own opinions or report what they've heard. Make notes of their answers. Report to the class what you found out. Would you recommend any of the restaurants?

MEMO

Lesson 2 A Night at the Movies

A Model Conversation

Read the conversation. Then listen. Complete the exercise below. Track 14

Chad: I heard you had your first date with Rob on Saturday. How did it go?

Angela: Not bad, but it didn't go totally smoothly.

Chad: Uh-oh. What happened? You went to the movies, right?

Angela: Yeah. I booked the tickets online for the 7 o'clock showing at the Sunrise Theater downtown. We agreed to meet there early so we could have coffee first. But by ten to seven, Rob hadn't shown up. And my cell phone had died.

Chad: Oh, no. What did you do?

Angela: The guy at the box office let me charge my phone, and I called Rob. He'd gone to the wrong theater.

Chad: Ah, he went to the Sunrise Theater at the mall, didn't he?

Angela: Exactly. So I told him to hurry and meet me downtown. By the time he arrived, the movie had started. We missed the first ten minutes.

Chad: I bet Rob was upset.

Angela: He was pretty embarrassed. But the movie was funny, so he'd cheered up by the end.

Number these events from 1 to 5 in the order that they happened.

____ Angela called Rob. ____ Rob arrived at the right theater.

____ The movie started. ____ It was 6:50. ____ Angela charged her phone.

B Vocabulary

Write the words and phrases from the box next to the correct definitions.

smoothly	showing	box office	mall	hurry	exactly	embarrassed	cheer up

1. ____________________ to move, go, or act quickly
2. ____________________ feeling confused and silly in front of other people
3. ____________________ without problems or difficulties
4. ____________________ to start to feel happier; to be in a better mood
5. ____________________ a large building with many kinds of stores inside
6. ____________________ the act of making a movie, TV show, etc., available for people to see
7. ____________________ a word used to say that someone is correct or that you agree completely
8. ____________________ the place at a theater where people buy tickets

C About You

Think about the last movie you saw at a movie theater. Discuss the following questions with a partner.

- What kind of movie was it, and what was the title?
- Where did you see it?
- Who did you see it with?
- How did you purchase the tickets to this show?
- Would you recommend this movie to others? Why or why not?

D Grammar

Past perfect tense

Brief note

The past perfect clause can also come first. No comma is needed in that case.
*The movie **had started** by the time he arrived.*

past perfect	
The past perfect tense is used to talk about an action that was finished before something else happened in the past. The past perfect has the form *had* + past participle. *Had* is often shortened to *-'d* after pronouns.	
the action happened before a specific past time (often with *at/by* + time)	He didn't show up. It was five to seven (then). → At five to seven, he **hadn't shown up**.
	It stopped raining before 4:30. → By 4:30, it **had stopped** raining.
the action happened before a specific event (often with a simple past clause using *by the time* or *when*)	They went to bed. Then I got home. → When I got home, they **had** / they**'d** (already) **gone** to bed.
	The movie started. Then he arrived. → By the time he arrived, the movie **had** (already) started.

E Grammar Practice

Circle the correct answers.

1. Josephine still (didn't call / hadn't called) by 11 o'clock last night.
2. A: Why didn't Max join you for the movie last night?
   B: He'd already (saw / seen) it.
3. By the time we left the theater, the sun (came / had come) out.
4. When I (met / had met) my friend at the box office, (she / she'd) already bought the tickets.

Combine the sentences using the words in parentheses and the past perfect.

5. He spent all his money. Then we left the mall. (by the time)

   ____

6. We didn't eat all our popcorn. Then the movie ended. (when)

   ____

7. You started eating. Then I walked into the restaurant. (when, already)

   ____

F Listen to Write

You are at a movie theater box office waiting for a friend. You have already bought tickets. Then you hear an announcement about the film you were going to see. Listen to the announcement and then write a text to your friend explaining the problem. Track 15

MEMO

⋆ Unit 6 • About Me ⋆

Lesson 1 My Personality

A Warm-up

Talk about the questions as a class.

1. Do you know anyone who is an extrovert?
2. Do you know anyone who is an introvert?
3. Do you know anyone who is an ambivert?
4. Which word best describes your personality?

B Authentic Text

1 Read and circle the words that can be used to describe someone's personality. Then answer the questions. Track 16

Paragraph 1

Everyone has a different personality. Some people are lively and social, while others are shy and quiet. Scientists describe people who love being in groups as extroverted. They describe people who prefer to be alone as introverted.

Paragraph 2

Extroverts like being the center of attention and do well in most social situations. They are comfortable at parties and become bored when they are alone. Extroverts communicate well and appear to be friendly, charming, and approachable. These qualities make extroverts excellent salespeople, event planners, financial advisers, and even hairstylists.

Paragraph 3

Often described as loners, introverts prefer spending time engaged in their own interests. Some people believe introverts are never confident, but that belief is not true. Many introverts are more comfortable listening than speaking. Introverts have many other good qualities. They are often more creative than extroverts, and they appear to be calmer and more thoughtful. Suitable careers for introverted people include scientific researchers, artists, photographers, programmers, and accountants.

Paragraph 4

Not everyone's character can be clearly defined as introverted or extroverted. Most people can be one or the other, depending on the situation. For this reason, many scientists argue for a third personality type: ambiverts. Ambiverts are people who can change between introversion and extroversion. They don't hate attention, but they also don't seek it out.

Brief note

The *center of attention* is someone who attracts the attention or interest of everyone in a group.

2 **Choose the best title for each paragraph.**

__________ I'm a Listener, Not a Talker

__________ Who I Am

__________ A Little Bit of Both

__________ Look at Me!

3 **Choose the four statements below that are true according to the information in the reading.**

1. ☐ People who feel more comfortable in social situations are extroverts.
2. ☐ Introverts are not very friendly.
3. ☐ Extroverts are not creative.
4. ☐ Extroverts make good salespeople.
5. ☐ Introverts are often called loners.
6. ☐ Introverts do not always lack confidence.

C Vocabulary

Put the words in the columns you think they belong in. You can use the words more than once. Discuss your answers as a class.

lively, social, shy, quiet, charming, confident, creative, calm, thoughtful, loner

Introvert	Ambivert	Extrovert

D Use the Language

Who would you like to go traveling with?

1 **You have won a free trip to one of the following destinations. Pick a location and two friends to take along. Then write a short description of your friends.**

Las Vegas

Lake Tahoe

Aspen

Friend #1

Name: ____________________

Hobbies/Interests:

____

Personality:

____

Friend #2

Name: ____________________

Hobbies/Interests:

____

Personality:

____

2 **Answer the questions. Discuss them as a class.**

1. Why would you bring Friend #1?

____

2. Why would you bring Friend #2?

____

3. Why did you choose ____________________ as your destination?

____

4. Do you think that your friends will like the destination? Why?

____

____

____

MEMO

Lesson 2 My Dreams

A Warm-up

Talk about the questions as a class.

1. What should people consider before choosing a career?
2. What considerations are most important to you?
3. What career are you considering?

B Audio

1 Listen and answer the questions below. Track 17

1. What is the main topic of the talk?
   a. changing careers
   b. following your dreams
   c. deciding on a profession

2. What is the main purpose of the talk?
   a. to persuade listeners to choose a certain career path
   b. to advise listeners on career decisions
   c. to inform listeners about the job market

3. Which is true about the speaker?
   a. She no longer sings.
   b. She used to dream of being a singer.
   c. She is now a professional singer.

4. What does the speaker say about the job market?
   a. It is always changing nowadays.
   b. It is currently bad for lawyers.
   c. It is not good for young people.

5. Why does the speaker say this?
   "Now I'm not saying you shouldn't have big dreams and ambitions—you should."
   a. to correct a mistake she had made earlier
   b. to suggest that listeners change their goals
   c. to express support for listeners' dreams

6. What did Joy do after losing her job?
   a. She started her own law firm.
   b. She looked for another law job.
   c. She studied for a new career.

2 Discuss the following questions as a class.

1. Who is probably the audience for the talk?
2. Why does the speaker talk about her friend Joy?
3. Do you think that the speaker gives good advice?

C Vocabulary

1 **Write the words from the box under the correct pictures.**

salary	various	profession	path	honest

1. ____________________

2. ____________________

3. ____________________

4. ____________________

5. ____________________

2 **Match the words and phrases with the correct definitions.**

1. obvious •	• a. having the qualities that are right, needed, or appropriate
2. talent •	• b. able to see things as they actually are; sensible
3. make a living •	• c. a plan to follow if the original one does not work
4. suitable •	• d. a special ability that allows someone to do something well
5. ambition •	• e. easy to see, notice, or understand
6. realistic •	• f. a desire to be successful; a particular goal or aim
7. plan B •	• g. to earn enough money to pay for your needs

D Grammar

Stative and continuous verb meanings

	stative	continuous
be	That's **not** a realistic movie. (fact)	You**'re not being** realistic. (current behavior/attitude)
feel	I **feel** that everything will be okay. (belief/opinion)	I**'m feeling** optimistic. (current feeling /attitude)
have	Brian **has** two dogs and a cat. (possession)	Brian is **having** a great time. (current action)
like/love*	I **like/love** to work with people. (likes/tastes)	I**'m liking/loving** my new job! (current enjoyment)
see	**Do** you **see** someone at the door? (sight)	**Have** you **been seeing** anyone? (dating)
think	Irina **thinks** we should celebrate. (belief/opinion)	Irina **is thinking** about having a party. (subject of current thoughts)
want**	I always **wanted** to visit Europe. (past, long-lasting, or permanent wish)	I**'ve been wanting** a vacation lately. (recent, temporary wish)

*The continuous use of *like* and *love* is informal. It is most common in the present continuous.
**The continuous use of *want* is most common in the present perfect continuous.

Fill in the blanks with the correct words from the box. Use the present continuous.

feel	love	be	see	think

1. I ____________ my classes this semester. They're really interesting.
2. Michelle and Kenji met at a party, and now they ____________ each other.
3. You've been quiet for a while. What ____________ you ____________ about?
4. I was sick yesterday, but now I ____________ much better.
5. What's the matter with Adam? He ____________ kind of cold and rude today.

E Use the Language

Career Aspirations

Think about your interests, talents, and personality. Then fill in the table below. Explain your choices to a partner.

My Dream Job	My Plan B	Other Suitable Jobs for Me (at least 3)

MEMO

★ Unit 7 · Finances ★

Lesson 1 Credit Cards

A Vocabulary

Look up the pronunciation and meaning of these words. Then listen. Track 18

interest

account

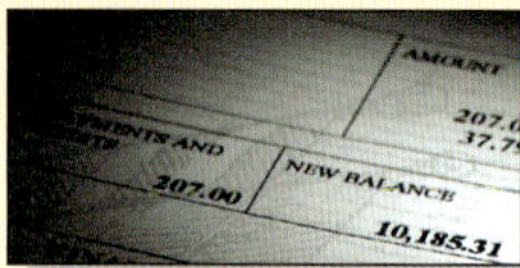

balance

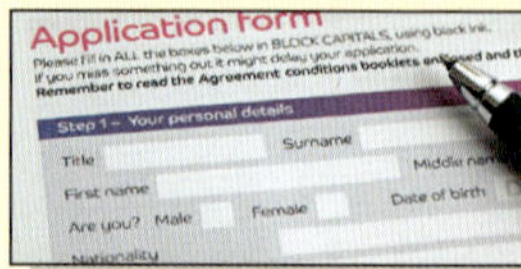

application

due date

transaction

monthly

payment

B Authentic Text

1 Read the credit card information and application.

Bank Today Silver Card

Application

FEES	
Annual Membership Fee	$0 fee for the first year; $75 every year after that
Transaction Fees	
Balance Transfer Fee	5% of the amount transferred; $5 minimum
Foreign Transaction Fee	None
Late Payment Fees	$15 if the balance is less than $100 $27 if the balance is between $100 and $300 $37 if the balance is more than $300

INTEREST CHARGES	
How to avoid paying interest on purchases	The due date will be 21 days after the date on your bill. You will not be charged interest on purchases if you pay your balance by the due date each month.
Minimum Interest Charge	None

First name Daniel	**Middle initial** L.	**Surname** Munroe	
Mailing address 1 335 19th St.		**Mailing address 2** Apt. 201	
City Springfield		**State** IA	**ZIP code** 50001

Check the types of accounts you own.	**Checking**	**Savings**
	✓	
Type of home	**Monthly housing payment**	
Apartment	$750.00	
Annual income $ 38,000.00		
Employer Worldwide Insurance, Inc.		

2 **Read the email and fill in the blanks with the correct words from the box.**

interest	minimum	avoid	membership	fees	account	monthly	transactions

Dear Mr. Munroe,

Your recent application for a Bank Today Silver Card has been accepted. Congratulations on your ❶ ______________! Your card will arrive at your mailing address within five business days. When you receive it, please call 1-888-9067 to confirm that you have your card and to activate it. Then you can begin making ❷ ______________.

You will receive a(n) ❸ ______________ bill in the mail. Each bill will state your current balance as well as the ❹ ______________ required payment for the preceding month. You can pay by check or online. With either option, we must receive at least the minimum payment on or before the due date. In this way, you can ❺ ______________ paying late ❻ ______________. But remember that if you pay your whole balance every month, you will not have to pay ❼ ______________ on your transactions.

If you have any questions, please contact us. You can also manage your ❽ ______________ online at BankToday.com.

Sincerely,

Bank Today Customer Service

C Grammar

Each, every, either, neither

Brief note

Each, *either*, and *neither* can also be used alone as pronouns:
Each *receives a bill.* ***Either*** *is fine.* ***Neither*** *charges an annual fee.*

each, every, either, neither

The words *each*, *every*, *either*, and *neither* can come before singular countable nouns. *Each*, *either*, and *neither* can also come before pronouns, but must be followed by *of*. Before plural nouns, they must be followed by *of* + determiner.

	meaning	before a singular noun	before a plural noun / pronoun
each	all the members of a group (focus on the individual)	I receive a bill **each** month.	**Each of their** customers receives a bill. **Each of** them receives a bill.
every	all the members of a group (focus on the group)	It's good to pay your bills **every** month.	
either	of two options: A or B	**Either** option for payment is fine.	**Either of the** options is fine. **Either of** them is fine.
neither	of two options: not A and not B	**Neither** bank charges an annual fee.	**Neither of the** banks charges an annual fee. **Neither of** them charges an annual fee.

Circle the correct words.

1. It's a good idea to have a different password for every (account / accounts) that you have.
2. I'm careful about (each / every) of my credit card purchases.
3. You can have fun shopping at either (the / of the) two department stores in town.
4. We accept all credit cards at this store, so you can use (either / neither) of those.

D Use the Language

Comparing Cards

Work with a partner. If you had to choose either of the credit cards below, which one would you choose? Explain your choice to the class.

	Mobile Bank Card	Shine Freedom Card
Interest	No interest for first 12 months; 10% after that	No interest for first 18 months; 18% after that
Annual fee	$80	None
Special offers	5% discount at most supermarkets	7% discount at popular restaurants and cafés

MEMO

Lesson 2 Financial Advice

A Warm-up

Talk about the questions as a class.

Has anyone ever given you advice about money? If so, who? Did you take the advice?

B Prewriting

Complete the table.

A purchase you wish you hadn't made	A major purchase you're happy with	Something you do to save money when shopping	A major purchase you want to make in the future

C Authentic Text

Read the article about financial advice.

Brief note
The idiom *a rainy day* refers to a time of difficulty or need.

Money Tips for Young People

By Lucy Quayle

I'm an accountant, and I've been advising young working adults about financial matters for fifteen years. Here are my most important tips on how to manage your money.

- **Keep some cash for emergencies.**
  Life is full of unpleasant surprises: illness, suddenly becoming unemployed, and other disasters. Therefore, it's a good idea to keep some money for a rainy day. I recommend keeping at least three months' worth of expenses saved for emergencies.
- **Make a monthly budget that includes savings and stick to it.**
  Make a plan for all of your expenses and do your best to follow the plan. Open a savings account and put some money in it each month. This is important for your future. Your monthly savings should be at least 10 percent of your income. Save more than that if you can afford it. However, this doesn't mean that you can't have fun. Be sure to budget some money for entertainment!
- **Avoid using credit cards too much.**
  When you're shopping, credit cards are more convenient than cash. But you shouldn't use them to spend money that you don't have. Many young people are addicted to charging items now and worrying about them later. Believe me—I understand! The problem is that you'll often regret it. I've heard this from my clients many times. Remember that the interest on your credit card balance is very expensive. If you already have credit card debt, don't add to it. Try to pay it off as soon as possible.

Brief note
To *charge* an item is to pay for it with a credit card.

D Analyze the Text

1 Read the statements and circle true or false.

1. You should save a year's worth of money for emergencies. true false
2. It is not a good idea to include plans for fun in your monthly budget. true false
3. You should save a minimum of 10 percent of your monthly income. true false
4. Young people should avoid using credit cards for any reason. true false
5. People often wish that they hadn't made purchases with a credit card. true false

2 Answer the questions with one or two complete sentences.

1. According to the writer, what are two emergencies that you might need money for?

____

____

2. What two pieces of advice does the writer give young people about credit cards?

____

____

E Vocabulary

1 Write the words from the box under the correct pictures.

accountant	illness	regret	financial	advise

1. ______________

2. ______________

3. ______________

4. ______________

5. ______________

2 **Fill in the blanks with the correct words from the box.**

matter	stick to	pay off	unemployed	emergency

1. Bryan made a diet plan to get healthier and lose weight, but he can't ________________ it.
2. When the economy is strong and growing, fewer people are ________________.
3. You should keep some money saved in case there is an ________________.
4. When I finally ________________ my student loans, I'm going to celebrate!
5. The manager said that there was an important ________________ to discuss.

B Role-Play

Work with a partner. Imagine that one of you wants to make a large purchase on a credit card and that the other thinks it's a bad idea. Make notes below. Role-play a conversation. Then perform it for the class.

Item(s) to be purchased		
Reasons for		
Reasons against		

MEMO

★ Unit 8 · Science ★

Lesson 1 Why We Love Science Fiction

A Warm-up

Talk about the questions as a class.

Have you read any science fiction stories or novels? Which ones? Who wrote them?

B Authentic Text

1 Read and listen to the magazine article. Then answer the questions below. Track 19

Why Do We Love Science Fiction?

By Ali Martin

Paragraph 1

People enjoy science fiction. Of the all-time top three box-office movies worldwide, at least two can be put into that category: *Avatar* (number one) and *Star Wars Episode VII: The Force Awakens* (number three). Science fiction is popular because it focuses on fascinating topics such as science, and relates to many people's greatest hopes and fears.

Brief note

A *submarine* is a boat that travels underwater.

Paragraph 2

Human beings love to learn about how the world works. Good science fiction not only entertains us, but also teaches us about scientific concepts. Jules Verne, the 19th-century French novelist, has been called "the father of science fiction." In 1870, he wrote *20,000 Leagues Under the Sea*, a novel about exploring the ocean in a submarine. At that time, submarines were a new invention. His book was praised by critics and interested the public in sea exploration. It even inspired the development of new, improved submarines.

Brief note

Aliens are living things from another planet.

Paragraph 3

We also love science fiction because it allows us to imagine all the exciting things that could happen someday. In the *Star Wars* series, space travel has progressed to an incredible level. Humans easily fly from planet to planet, and they socialize with aliens as if it were no big deal. What little kid hasn't dreamed about that? In these adventure stories, people use science to influence the future of mankind—in a good way.

Brief note

No big deal is a colloquial expression meaning "not important."

Paragraph 4

But science can be really frightening, too. At some point, most of us worry about nuclear weapons, aliens who take over Earth, or robots that rebel against the humans who invented them. In the classic film *Terminator*, for instance, technology gets out of control. A computer system begins to think for itself, and it threatens to destroy mankind with nuclear bombs. But a couple of heroes manage to save us all. Stories like this are terrifying and comforting at the same time. They help us to face our biggest fears and imagine how to defeat them.

2 **Talk about the questions after you read and listen.**

1. Have you seen the movies mentioned in the text? What other science fiction movies have you seen?
2. Does *20,000 Leagues Under the Sea* sound interesting to you? What other books is Jules Verne famous for?
3. What other positive things does science fiction predict about the future?
4. Which of the future threats mentioned in the text scares you the most?

3 **Choose the best title for each paragraph.**

________ A Big Box-Office Draw

________ Scary but Fun

________ Science Fiction as Education

________ We Can't Wait for the Future

4 **Circle the five statements below that are true according to the information in the reading.**

1. Some of the most popular movies of all time are science-fiction movies.
2. Jules Verne was an author who lived in the 1800s.
3. *20,000 Leagues Under the Sea* was written before submarines were invented.
4. Verne's book did not receive good reviews.
5. Some science fiction helps us imagine a future that is better than the present.
6. The *Star Wars* series is about a future that many kids dream about.
7. The movie *Terminator* is about a robot rebellion.
8. Movies like *Terminator* are not scary because we know the events could never happen.

C Vocabulary

1 **Write the words from the box under the correct pictures.**

nuclear	mankind	progress	threaten	socialize

1. ________ 2. ________ 3. ________ 4. ________ 5. ________

2 **Fill in the blanks with the correct words from the box.**

take over	face	concept	novelist	rebel

1. I understand the ________________ of time travel, but I don't see how it could work in practice.
2. If you have a serious problem, you can't ignore it. You must ________________ it and solve it.
3. It's normal for teenagers to ________________ against their parents.
4. In this movie, some terrorists ________________ an office building and demand money.
5. Charles Dickens was the most popular British ________________ of his time.

D Use the Language

You're the Novelist

Imagine the pictures below are the covers of science fiction novels. With a partner, come up with a title for each and make notes about the basic plot. Share your ideas with the class.

Title: **Plot:**	**Title:** **Plot:**	**Title:** **Plot:**

MEMO

Lesson 2 A Sci-Fi Story

A Warm-up

Talk about the questions as a class.

1. Do you prefer to read fiction or non-fiction? Why?
2. Have you ever tried creative writing (stories, plays, poems, etc.)?

B Prewriting

Good stories have a clear beginning, middle, and end. Think of one story you know from a science fiction book or movie. Make some notes about its beginning, middle, and end. Tell the story to a partner.

Beginning	Middle	End

C Authentic Text

1 Read the beginning of a science fiction short story (adapted from "The Crystal Egg" by H. G. Wells).

Track 20

The Crystal Egg

Mr. Cave was an old man who owned a little antique shop. The various items in his shop included old furniture, lamps, books, and toys. But he had a favorite item: It was a piece of bright crystal in the shape of an egg. Occasionally, someone offered to buy the lovely crystal egg, but Mr. Cave always raised the price until the customer gave up. That's because he felt strangely fascinated by the egg. This annoyed his wife, and he didn't understand it himself. He just didn't want to sell the egg.

Brief note

Antiques are objects that are old, and usually rare or beautiful.

Late one night, Mr. Cave couldn't sleep. Feeling bored, he was wandering around his shop, looking at the items on the shelves in the moonlight coming through the windows. He was quiet and careful so that he wouldn't disturb his sleeping wife upstairs. Then Mr. Cave noticed a soft ray of light across the room. It was coming from the crystal egg on the shelf, and a mysterious force seemed to be pulling him toward it. With great curiosity, he walked over, picked it up, and looked carefully at it. His eyes opened wide in amazement. He couldn't believe the sight that he saw inside the glowing egg…

Brief note

Glowing means "giving off a soft, warm light."

2 **Put a check mark (✓) next to the four correct statements. Then number them 1-4 in the order that they happened.**

1. ☐ ______ A bright light coming from the egg woke Mr. Cave up one night.
2. ☐ ______ He was walking around his store one night by himself.
3. ☐ ______ Although people wanted to buy the egg, Mr. Cave refused to sell it.
4. ☐ ______ The egg was producing light, which attracted his attention.
5. ☐ ______ He saw something amazing inside the crystal egg.
6. ☐ ______ Mr. Cave's wife didn't want him to sell the unusual item.

3 **Answer the questions in one or two complete sentences.**

1. Why hasn't anyone bought the crystal egg?

____

____

2. What emotions does Mr. Cave experience in the second paragraph?

____

____

D Vocabulary

1 **Write the words from the box under the correct pictures.**

crystal	moonlight	curiosity	ray	wander

1. ______________

2. ______________

3. ______________

4. ______________

5. ______________

2 **Circle the answers that are closest in meaning to the words in bold.**

1. I'm worried about him—he's been behaving **strangely** lately.

a. weirdly b. constantly c. badly

2. We enjoyed the kids' **amazement** as they watched the magic tricks.

a. humor b. surprise c. confusion

3. Suddenly, a **mysterious** light appears in the sky. Could it be an alien ship?

a. unknown b. effective c. beautiful

4. I hate to be **disturbed** while I'm studying, so I lock my bedroom door.

a. questioned b. bothered c. corrected

5. Gravity is the **force** that causes objects to fall when you drop them.

a. concept b. rule c. power

E Use the Language

Finish the Sci-fi Story

Read the writing guide. Then, on a separate sheet of paper, work with one or two partners to complete "The Crystal Egg" with your own ideas. Write at least six sentences. Share your story with the class.

Writing Guide

In creative writing, it is important for a story to have a beginning, middle, and end. It is also important to create a picture in the reader's mind. Here is how to finish the short story.

1. **What does Mr. Cave see?** Continue the story: What does he see in the crystal egg that amazes him? Use adjectives and adverbs to describe it. Help the reader to "see" what Mr. Cave sees.
2. **What happens next?** This is the middle of the story. Use action verbs to describe the event(s) that result from Mr. Cave's vision in the crystal egg. These must be interesting enough so that readers want to keep reading. Use real scientific concepts in your story if possible.
3. **How does the story end?** Readers like to know exactly what happens to the characters at the end of a story. Satisfy their curiosity by stating what happens to Mr. Cave, his wife, and the egg. It may be a happy, sad, scary, funny, or surprising ending. Use your imagination.

MEMO